Mick Bensley
May '90

WATERCOLOURS OF NORFOLK PAST

WATERCOLOURS OF NORFOLK PAST

by Mick Bensley

Verse by David Corran

S.B. Publications

1990

For Aimee

First published in 1990 by S.B. Publications
5 Queen Margaret's Road, Loggerheads, Nr. Market Drayton, Shropshire, TF9 4EP

Design and typography by Mick Bensley

Illustrations ©Copyright 1990 Mick Bensley
Text ©Copyright 1990 David Corran

British Library Cataloguing in Publication Data
Bensley, Michael. Watercolours of Norfolk past.
1. Norfolk, history. I. Title. II. Corran, David. 942.61
ISBN 1-870708-40-7   ISBN 1-870708-41-5 pbk

Typeset in Palatino and
printed in England by Witley Press Ltd., Hunstanton, Norfolk.

CONTENTS

CONTENTS

FOREWORD

The publication of a book of Mick's paintings is long overdue and will be greatly welcomed by his large and increasing following in both his native Norfolk as well as further afield.

It is some years since I was first introduced to Mick's work, a lifeboat rescue that captured the danger and tension as the boat drew alongside a stricken vessel; the breaking sea seemed so real that you could smell the salt in the air.

It was in the years to come as an admirer, then collector and publisher that I was to work closely with the artist. It was then that I began to understand how the painstaking research, the study of old photographs and prints, and the many chats with local people all contribute to the creation of one of his paintings.

A Sheringham fisherman recently told me that Mick was the only artist he knew who could paint a crab boat which could be recognised without reference to the name, such is his skill. Seascapes, river scenes and the Norfolk countryside in their many moods always feature in Mick's annual exhibitions.

In this collection there are examples of the artist's finest work, reconstructing days long past and presented with great care to rekindle the atmosphere of those days when the pace of life was slower.

I am truly pleased that Mick's work will now be seen by a wider public and receive the recognition which his talent deserves.

Tim Groves
In the Picture, Holt. January 1990.

INTRODUCTION

Norfolk has experienced considerable change since the last century. Buildings, many of the ways of life and even the landscape have changed. But the county's unique character remains.

Contrary to popular belief, Norfolk is not flat. There are the undulations of the North and West, the marshlands, sand dunes and cliffs — always under threat of erosion — lush meadows, open heathland, forests and the broads. A variety of landscapes beneath characteristic wide open skies which have always proved an inspiration for countless artists.

It's no surprise that a county with Norfolk's long and open coastline has a strong maritime heritage. Generations have gone to sea to earn their living, or served in the lifeboat service whose proud and distinguished record in saving many lives bears testimony to the bravery of the men facing these dangerous waters.

This book contains thirty-four timeless land and seascapes painted by Mick Bensley who has lived in Norfolk for most of his life. The paintings provide a nostalgic view of this beautiful county and reflect the traditions and heritage of a bygone age.

Commencing at King's Lynn, the paintings feature the North Norfolk coastline, Great Yarmouth, the Norfolk Broads, Norwich and end at the Suffolk border.

To accompany each painting, David Corran has written short verse which perfectly captures the mood and beauty of the paintings.

the
PLATES

The Purfleet, King's Lynn, in the early 1900s
Watercolour 16 × 24 ins 1989

The Customs House
with unchanging face
for three hundred years
has witnessed the pace
of the coming and going,
the to-ing and fro-ing,
the ebbing and flowing
of people and boats,
of cargoes afloat:
all change:
on Purfleet, King's Lynn.

Moonlight on the River Ouse, King's Lynn
Watercolour 12 × 24 ins 1989

A hand on the tiller
to steer the way
  and a lambent light
    to see
and a gentle breeze
  which fills the sails.
  The port's in sight
    as daylight fails,
King's Lynn —
    harbour and home.

Brancaster Staithe
Watercolour 14 × 20 ins 1987

Like a world in limbo;
Where the cyclic advance
of the tide holds the balance
of life on the margins
of land —
at the edge
of the sea.

Goggs Mill, Hempton, near Fakenham
Watercolour 10 × 16 ins 1990

*Outwardly
settled
though standing
by water.*

*Inwardly
mill wheels
turn constant
in motion.*

*Harmonic
union
of wood, brick
and mortar.*

The Mediaeval Pumphouse, Walsingham
Watercolour 11 × 13 ins 1990

How many pilgrims
wearied by road,
how many horses
bent but unbowed
over how many years
when unburdened of load
have slaked their thirst here
where blessed waters have flowed?

Unloading, Blakeney Quay in the 1880s
Watercolour 12 × 20 ins 1989

A place of meeting
of cart
and barge
of drayman
and boatman.
Where labours exchange
from floating
to rumbling.
At Blakeney,
down by the old quay.

13

Coastal traders, Blakeney Quay
Watercolour 12 × 24 ins 1989

Stand now quiet
at the quay
and hear sounding clear
the echo of lays
sung in halcyon days
and creaking and clatter
of wheels as they turn,
the banter and chatter
of deals struck and done.
When it seemed that the world
and his friend had to come
to Blakeney.

Langham in the grip of winter
Watercolour 9 × 14 ins 1989

Grey scudding clouds
chase over the sky
and scatter light
on racing by
as chimney smoke
whipped hereabout
signals warmth within
and cold without.

Cley Mill, morning light
Watercolour 12 × 24 ins 1989

Over the sea
and across the land,
over tufted mounds
and banks of sand,
blows the East wind
which is caught
in the four-fingered span
of Cley Mill.

Salthouse Dyke
Watercolour 11 × 17 ins 1989

As successive floods
draw back,
there remains ever less
historic village,
whose doughty spirit
and resolute presence
await the next
North Sea offence
yet still stands proud
despite stretched defence
until the day
when it's washed away.

21

After the rain, Upper Sheringham Church
Watercolour 11½ × 19½ ins 1985

Autumn rain,
following showers
of leaves,
falls to fill
every hollow.
It's pitter
and patter
grows gradually quieter,
slowing till ceased.
Then peace . . . reigns.

First of the herring, Sheringham beach
Watercolour 12 × 20 ins 1988

Beneath a moon's
cool light,
expectations
in the night.
For,
like quicksilver
in wicker,
the first herring on
Sheringham
shore has arrived.

25

Sheringham fishermen getting away at dawn
Watercolour 12 × 20 ins 1988

As grey shades
of dawn yield
to colours
of daylight,
the fishermen
of Sheringham
load shingle
as ballast
whilst holding
boats steadfast.
They're ready
for launch.

Crab boat beaching in squally weather, Sheringham
Watercolour 10 × 15 ins 1987

Emerging from silence
waves fill to white heights
dash down on the shingle,
seep deep,
draw hard
and hiss in retreat.

Threat at its greatest
when steering to shore.
The junction of elements
draws strength
from men
well versed in Sea Lore.

Sheringham Lifeboat Henry Ramey Upcher
taking the crew of the Norwegian brig Ispolen, c.1897
Watercolour 18 × 25 ins 1987

Cold to numb the stoutest heart
Blew hard across a frenzied sea
Shrieking round the stranded brig,
A plight all eyes ashore could see.
But there, equipped with oil skins
Cork belts and resolute will,
Pitting their strength against an ebbing tide
And steeling themselves to risks they knew,
The redoubtable men, hardy beachmen,
Put out, pulled hard and saved the crew.

31

Cromer, edge of Poppyland
Watercolour 16 × 24 ins 1989

When I return
to my coastal home,
where open cliff-tops
offer space to roam,
I look for the signs
of my yesterdays,
seeking out the unchanged,
where my memories lay.
And there I find waving
in blushed familiarity,
a field of red poppies
in splendid reality.

Cromer crab boats heading for home
Watercolour 13 × 20 ins 1988

The men of Cromer,
like scattered specks
of toiling humanity
embraced by their Sea's
familiar enormity,
work to a code
of seasoned humility
all within sight
of St. Peter and Paul's.

Colliers on Cromer beach
Watercolour 12 × 24 ins 1989

As the age
of coastal trade
comes to end,
the old comrades
lie together
on the sands
of low water
and side by side stand
in quiet reflection.

They fuel the town
with coal from the North,
awaiting the turn
of the tide
which will take them away.
Yet as they set sail,
a question will stay,

'When shall we three meet again?'

Launching a yawl off Caister beach
Watercolour 16 × 26 ins 1990

Between the cry of the wind
and the roar of the sea.

Instructions are hailed
the ballast is placed,
the mizen is hoisted
and shoulders are braced.
The sett is applied
by men ready to push.
Then the order is given
and she's launched with a rush.

39

Leaving Yarmouth harbour
Watercolour 12 × 20 ins 1989

Beneath the gaze
of tiered windows
a lone barge
glides up
an ambling Yare.
The slap of water
and flap of sail
bode well
and farewell,
it's leaving harbour.

The River Bure, Great Yarmouth
Watercolour 10 × 16 ins 1990

*And perhaps it seemed
work never would cease.*

*Once a Waterman's frontier
not far from where
the Bure met the Yare
and transfer was made
between inland and coastal
vessels of trade.*

*But since that time
the weight of traffic
has shifted from river to road.
The old bridge now replaced
by one larger, concrete based
to carry its increased load.*

*But the river still flows
in relative peace.*

The fishing fleet returning, Gorleston Pier
Watercolour 10 × 16 ins 1989

Hear times change
as the cry of gulls
heralds not
the whip of sails,
but the pulse of steam.
Boats with power within
plough down the coast
with much to win.
First back, top price,
at market.

Fishing smacks in the North Sea
Watercolour 14 × 9 ins 1988

Becalmed in a breathless pall
then beset by a driving squall
smacks trawl
a living.
Enduring the sting of salt spray
whilst by night and by day
they stay
at sea
the threat to life
but supporter of living.

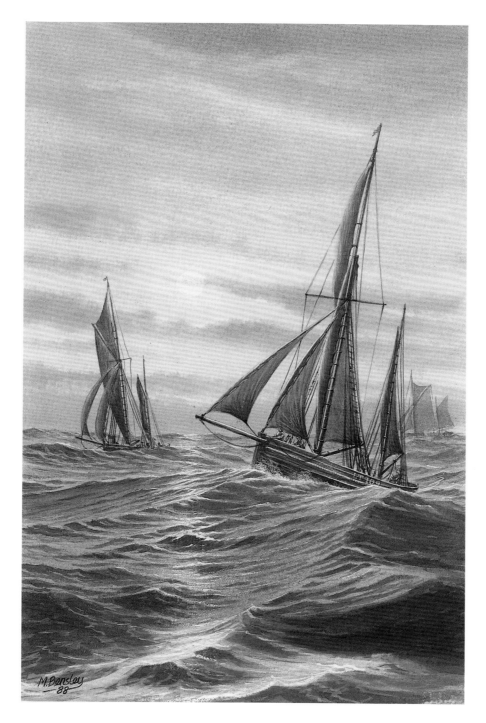

Pleasure wherry on South Walsham Broad
Watercolour 10 × 20 ins 1989

Enjoying a cruise
on a sun-flecked Broad
full of magic, romance
and pleasure.
Two people are here
who will remember their hour
as one couple, fulfilled
and together.

Changing weather, Thurne Dyke
Watercolour 9 × 18 ins 1989

And winds blow change.
Slanting rain in sweeping veils
of crowding darkness
    as sunlight fails.
    And, winds blow motion.
In differing ways
    as wet winds wail
their aerial might
    is harnessed by sail.

Wherry about to negotiate Acle bridge
Watercolour 12 × 20 ins 1989

Where once was a ford,
three arches now focus
all movement of trade,
which over goes
and under flows
the old stone bridge,
bestriding the river —
and spanning the years.

Buxton Lock on the upper Bure
Watercolour 16 × 14 ins 1989

As things once were . . .

To serve the needs
of trading folk
a lock
where wherries rose
in turbulent flows
and levels equate
about the gate
at Buxton.

. . . now nothing's there.

Towards the end of the day, near Buxton
Watercolour 14 × 9 ins 1989

November is closing
as Novembers of old
crisp light still shines sharply
in seasonal cold.

Farm wheels are in motion
gulls cry as they poach.
Life's sounds surround Buxton
in winter's approach.

57

57

Horstead mill around the turn of the century
Watercolour 17 × 13 ins 1990

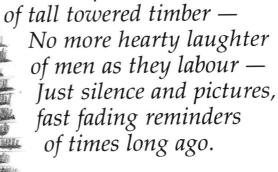

No longer the rumble
and hum of mill wheels
in full flow.
And gone is the splendour
of tall towered timber —
No more hearty laughter
of men as they labour —
Just silence and pictures,
fast fading reminders
of times long ago.

Wroxham Regatta
Watercolour 15 × 23 ins 1989

A panoply of canvas
tall masts
and full blown sail.
In expectation,
relaxation,
well scrubbed down
then dressed up.
Community afloat,
yachts, rowing boats
and bedizened pleasure wherries.

61

Trading Wherries on the River Wenum, Norwich
Watercolour 12 × 20 ins 1989

Broken but unbowed
stand still
the defences of old,
as the trade of the day
makes waves
plies its way
to Norwich and goods
bought and sold.

63

The old watermen's quarter, River Wensum, Norwich
Watercolour 16 × 20 ins 1989

Rooftops and chimneys,
windows and doors,
tall masts and rigging
and goods in dry stores,
black sailed wherries
and small rowing boats
glide over the water,
their business afloat.

All crowded together
in a watery mews,
there's no lack of gossip
of scandal and news.
The wide world reflected
in so tiny a place,
where the people who work
also live face to face.

Beccles, from the Norfolk side
Watercolour 11 × 18 ins 1990

The lightest of breezes
in September air
imparts living movement
to the riverside where
it also draws effort
from bargemen who find
their strength's put to sweeping
when there's none in the wind.

Garboldisham Post Mill
Watercolour 16 × 14 ins 1989

Withstanding
the test of time
and adapted to turn
to face
the wind of every season.
With sails well trimmed
and twice cyclic motion
Garboldisham,
an art in revolution.

ACKNOWLEDGEMENTS

Thanks are due to the following who have lent paintings for reproduction in this book:

G. Refoy
"Cromer, edge of Poppyland"

L. Sheridan
"Colliers on Cromer beach"

M. Crowe
"Sheringham crab boats getting away at dawn"
"Crab boat beaching in squally weather"

M. Sidebotham
"After the rain, Upper Sheringham Church"

Tim Groves
"First of the herring, Sheringham beach"
"Rescue from Ispolen"

June & David Elliot
"Brancaster Staithe"

The following are in private collections:

"Morning light, Cley Mill";
"Unloading, Blakeney Quay";
"Crab boats off Cromer"; "Salthouse Dyke";
"Smacks in the North Sea";
"Fishing fleet returning"; "Thurne Dyke";
"Langham in the grip of winter";
"Coastal traders at Blakeney Quay";
"Wherry about to negotiate Acle bridge"; and
"November afternoon near Buxton"

Thanks also to:
Annie Quigg for typing the text and
Heather for reading it.

Chromatics (Brighton) and Focalpoint (Norwich) for the trannies.

And a special thanks to Aimee for advising me on the colour of certain horses.

BIBLIOGRAPHY

Brooks, P., *Cley living with memories of greatness*, Poppyland Publishing, 1984.

Brooks, P., *Have you heard about Blakeney?*, Poppyland Publishing, 1985.

Brooks, P., *Salthouse village of character and history*, Poppyland Publishing, 1984.

Dutt, W., *The Norfolk Broads*, Methuen, 1903.

Finch, R., and Benham, H., *Sailing Craft of East Anglia*, Terence Dalton Ltd., 1987.

Grint, B., *An Acle Chronicle*, Poppyland Publishing, 1989.

Harrod, W. and Linnell, C., *Norfolk: a Shell Guide*, Faber and Faber, 1960.

Higgins, D., *The Beachmen*, Terence Dalton Ltd., 1987.

Jennings, P., *Sun Pictures of the Norfolk Broads*, 1897.

Jones, E., *Poppyland in Pictures*, Poppyland Publishing, 1983.

Malster, R., *Wherries and Waterways*, Terence Dalton Ltd., 1986.

Sailing fishermen in old photographs, text by Elliot, C., Tops'l Books, 1978.

Simper, R., *East Coast Sail: working sail 1850-1970*, David and Charles, 1972.

Stibbons, P., Lee, K. and Warren, M., *Crabs and Shannocks: the longshore fishermen of North Norfolk*, Poppyland Publishing, 1983.

Tooke, C., *Caister beach boats and beachmen*, Poppyland Publishing, 1986.

Warren, M., *Cromer the chronicle of a watering place*, Poppyland Publishing, 1988.

Limited Edition Prints

The following plates in this book are also available as signed limited edition prints of 850 copies:

> Blakeney Quay, Image area 275 × 456 mm
> Cley Mill, Image area 265 × 530 mm
> Leaving Harbour, Image area 289 × 480mm

to be published as limited editions in 1990:

> Trading Wherries
> The Regatta

All enquiries should be addressed to:

**In the Picture
Fine Art Publishers
Unit 36, Sheringham Industrial Estate,
Weybourne Road, Sheringham,
Norfolk, NR26 8HF. (0263) 822265.**

Original Paintings and Limited Editions are always on display at our gallery:

**In the Picture
16, Chapel Yard, Holt, Norfolk.
(0263) 713720.**

MICK BENSLEY was born in Sheringham on the North Norfolk coast. He trained at the Norwich School of Art and then spent fifteen years working in London where he soon established himself as a Commercial Artist. He returned to Sheringham in 1980 to develop his career as a watercolour artist. In 1988 he moved to Brighton, alternating his work as a graphic designer and painting his beloved Norfolk. His work includes Norfolk landscapes, lifeboat rescues and reconstructions of bygone days.

DAVID CORRAN has studied physics and geography, qualified as a teacher, skied, played tennis, excelled at 'Trivial Pursuit', painted, written poetry, edited a video, filed architectural drawings and played guitar in a band.

He is currently an advertising copywriter.

Front cover: Colliers on Cromer beach
Back cover: The Medieval Pumphouse, Walsingham